CARMI BLACKSTOCK

WRITE AND GROW RICH

The Essential Guide on How to Do Copywriting Like a Pro, Discover How Effective Copywriting Can Get You To Earn Six Figures

Descrierea CIP a Bibliotecii Naţionale a României
CARMI BLACKSTOCK
   WRITE AND GROW RICH. The Essential Guide on How
to Do Copywriting Like a Pro, Discover How Effective
Copywriting Can Get You To Earn Six Figures / Carmi
Blackstock – Bucharest: Editura My Ebook, 2020
   ISBN

CARMI BLACKSTOCK

WRITE AND GROW RICH

The Essential Guide on How to Do Copywriting Like a Pro, Discover How Effective Copywriting Can Get You To Earn Six Figures

My Ebook Publishing House
Bucharest, 2020

TABLE OF CONTENTS

What is Copywriting & Why Is It So Important?

To answer the second part first: copywriting is perhaps the single most important skill in online marketing. Get it right and everything else will follow – sales, sign-ups, etc.

Get it wrong, and nothing else matters.

Simply put, copywriting is the writing you use to promote your online business. This can include your newsletter advertising messages, product sales information on your website and articles that promote your product. It's also your headlines, your ads - any writing you use to promote your website or product is what's known as copywriting.

Copywriting is what you use to get your customers and potential customers to take a particular action. For example:

Click on an ad

Place an order

Sign up for your mailing list

Click an affiliate link

Get them to refer a friend to your business

Many online business owners make the mistake of thinking they can just get some traffic and they'll be set. Those of you who are getting traffic without results know the folly of this.

I'd like to congratulate you for taking the time to read this guide because the information in it will put you ahead of many other internet business owners who make the mistake of thinking that copywriting isn't important.

Consider this:

When people visit your website, **you aren't there** to answer their questions, explain benefits, or to convince them how great your product is. Your words need to do that for you. In other words, you need effective copywriting - and that's exactly what I'm going to show in this guide.

The Basics of Copywriting: Important Concepts & Terms

In this chapter, we'll go over some concepts & terminology that will help you in understanding the principles of copywriting.

Read each one in detail. Along with the definitions, I've also added:

Examples and further detail for deeper understanding of these important concepts.

Exercises to apply these concepts.

This information will help give you a foundation for all the copywriting you do for your business. Even if you are familiar with some of the terminology, going through this chapter will give you a deeper understanding.

Target Market:

What does "Target Market" have to do with copywriting? Everything.

Your target market is the group of people you're soliciting, or selling your product to. Without a clear 'target' to write to, you can't be as effective as you would be when you're addressing a specific individual.

The more specific you are when you define your target market, the more effective your copywriting is going to be. Thinking of a target market as "women" or "moms" for instance, or even "pet owners", is too vague.

What women? Which moms? Which pet owners?

> *Persona's*
>
> *The concept of "Persona's" is used extensively in the marketing & advertising industries.*
>
> *From Wikipedia: "In marketing, personas are fictional characters created to represent the different user types within a targeted demographic, attitude and/or behavior set that might use a site, brand or product in a similar way"*
>
> *By addressing a specific "Persona", you can focus your copywriting very directly, and very effectively.*

When defining your target market, you want to take into account as many considerations as possible. There are many, many different factors that can make up your specific target market.

For example:

Age

Income

Interests

If it's a woman, her marital status may come into play

If it's moms, you might want to have an idea about the age of her children; if she works outside the home, etc.

If it's a pet owner, what kind of pet she has, what breed, etc.

In the advertising industry, there is something called "Persona's".

Wants, wishes and desires *

Problems she needs solved *

---

*These last two are particular important because this is what really motivates people to spend their money and buy products. Yes, they buy to satisfy their immediate needs, but desire is what drives people to spend their money readily.

To help you further, here are some important human motivators that effect decision-making. Considering them in terms of your target market will help you in understanding what motivates your readers to take action:

Fear

Exclusivity

Guilt

Greed

Need for approval

Convenience

Pleasure

Some people might see it as unethical to play on the emotions of their potential customer, but you can use this information to really understand what motivates your target market and do it within your levels of comfort. After all, being a Copywriting Wizard means really finding the right customer for your product and showing them how they'll benefit from using it.

The more you understand your target market, the easier it will be to sell to them, and this will help you to understand their point-of-view, the problems they have, and how much they'd like a solution.

The Problem with Being Too Vague:

I've seen so many Internet marketers who try the vague "be everything to everyone" approach and it's really tough to make that work as a small business owner.

Consider a business that sells candles, or cosmetics; the vague "all things" approach business owner probably considers their target market to be simply women. The problem is, if you sell those things, not all women are your target.

Let look at that a little further…

There are plenty of women who don't care much about candles and they're content buying the typical drugstore cosmetics or no cosmetics at all. Those women are not the target market for that business.

Even a woman who thinks candles are lovely and wears a little makeup now and then, but doesn't readily spend her money on those items, is not the true target market.

That business needs to understand the woman who really wants to buy their product, and then she'll buy it **over and over again**.

Imagine Your Typical Customer:

> ### The Power Of Personas
>
> *Imagine if you could craft your message – customize it – precisely to the specific person who's reading it...*
>
> *That's the power of Personas – done properly, you are doing just that: 'customizing' your message specifically to the person reading*

What are his/her wants and desires? What problems does he/she need solved? If you don't already know that, try surveying the customers that you already have. Ask them a few questions about themselves, why they bought the product, what they like about it and what they don't like. In return, offer them a coupon or a discount to get that feedback. That information will be hugely valuable to you.

Think about your product:

What is the single most important reason your target audience would want to buy it? You need to be able to empathize with your target market, identify their problems and show how your product solves that problem. If you think too

14

generally about your target market, the passion is lost in your copy and it's tough to get anyone excited about anything.

Here again, a well fleshed-out 'Persona' will help you.

Suppose you sell an ebook about getting rid of acne and you simply talk about the embarrassment of acne; you might get some sales. But if you know that your target market for a specific ad campaign is teenagers, you might talk about being teased at school, worrying that they won't find a date and having a case study of a teenager who overcame that – now your copywriting will be much more powerful.

Here are a few more examples to illustrate how your target market is important and how it can vary from product-to-product and ad campaign to ad campaign:

If you sell more than one product and they're related (example: skin cream and eye shadow), each product that you sell can have a slightly or even a very different market. If the skin cream helps reduce wrinkles and the eye shadow is in a sparkly blue color, it's likely the skin cream will appeal to a woman into her 30s who would like to reduce wrinkles. The sparkly blue eye shadow is more likely to be appreciated by a younger, more trendy audience. Of course, there are exceptions and if you sell make-up, you have the opportunity to know your market best. Regardless, even within your own product line, you can identify differences in your target market and your copy should reflect this.

It is also possible that you have more than one very targeted market for an individual product!

If that's the case, you can create different promotional materials and sales pages to target those specific audiences. For example, if you sell that wrinkle cream and discover that not only are certain types of women buying the cream, but men are interested too, you can create promotional materials to target the problems and interests of each group. That way, when you have different advertising campaigns or promotions, you can send people the appropriate marketing materials.

You will sell more to a highly-targeted group of people than trying a lukewarm approach with the public in general. Leave general marketing to Amazon.com, Wal-Mart and other huge companies.

Note – Here's a Big Company That Does It Right: We mention Amazon.com and yes, they target a general audience overall with a wide variety of products, but a visit to their website will show you they customize their marketing right down to the individual visiting their website. They will show you like items based on what you are looking at on their site and

16

they remember this the next time you visit and try to offer you complimentary items. They are about as specific in their marketing as they can get.

Exercise: Start writing a list of all the characteristics of your typical customer. Use information gathered from customer surveys, as mentioned earlier in this section, and write at least 15-20 specific characteristics. This list will help you as you make your way through this guide.

USP:

USP stands for Unique Selling Position and this is what sets you apart from your competition. Put another way, a USP is some unique thing you offer that your competition is not offering. Here are just a few examples of a USP. Your USP will likely be very different:

Are you the only company that offers an unlimited time money back guarantee?

Do you cater to vegetarians when nobody else in your industry does?

Do you know the secret to a perfectly baked soufflé; what do you do that's different?

Do you look for hard-to-find items for your clients in 24 hours or less?

USP is a concept that is often difficult for people because every business is different. You need to really sit down, brainstorm and figure out your USP because if you don't, it's hard to stand out from the crowd and compete in your market.

Warning: A lot of home businesses make the mistake of making their low price as the USP. The problem is trying to sell for the lowest price is not often a profitable business model, especially for small home businesses like you. If you're not buying and selling in huge volumes it's just not worth it. Again, let's leave this kind of marketing to large companies like Wal-Mart or Amazon. They can afford it.

Some of the best customers you can ever have, don't worry about price. In my experience, the best customers are the ones who are more concerned about quality, exceptional service or that just buy because they plain old trust you and feel you understand them. As a home business owner with a smaller budget, you don't need to deal with bargain hunters.

Here is one of the most important questions you'll ask yourself when formulating your USP:

"Why would my customer buy my product instead of a competitor's?"

Think of what information or education you can provide to people who use your products. Go the extra mile where other big companies may not. Find something different than competing on price because trying to offer the lowest price will likely put you out of business. You want to price your products to receive a decent profit. That way, you'll need fewer sales to make just as much or more money.

Exercise: Make a list of 5-10 competitors and identify their USP. See how you compare to these companies and their USP. For example, if one company's USP is that they have the fastest delivery rates, are you able to compete with that? If another company offers the longest hours of service, are you able to compete with that? If there is a USP where you can outperform your competitor, you might want to pursue that option or you may still want to carve out your own unique position in the market.

Even if you think you've found your USP, continue the exercise, by giving yourself 5 minutes to write down what is

19

special about your products, service, etc. You can even invite family members and friends who know your business well to join in this brainstorming. Look at the lists and see what other unique things you can find that might just help you net more customers than one of your competitors.

Features:

You probably already have some idea what this word means. It basically describes what your product looks like, how it functions, etc. It is the basic information about your product.

Although features may be important to your potential customers, it's the benefits that will make them want to buy your product.

Exercise: Write down all the features of your product. Include every single detail from color to size to function. You can't write too much for this exercise so write it ALL down.

Benefits:

Benefits are the advantages your customer receives from using your product. As mentioned in the definition of features, in most cases, benefits will sell your products better than a feature does. Although successful copy combines both, the best copy for most products focuses on the benefits.

An example: You sell a ballpoint pen.

The features are black ink, a felt tip, and it comes with a lid.

The benefits are that it reduces hand cramping and eliminates smudges.

Notice how when I talked about the features of the pen, it sounds like any other pen, but when we talk about benefits, it make the pen sound more interesting. Those are benefits and they help sell your product. People have a problem and they want to solve it by buying your product. Show them the benefits of your product.

What If Your Customers Care About Features?

Sometimes, you might sell a product where customers heavily compare features. One example of this might be Internet service for businesses. Businesses who need an Internet connection want to know the rates, the speed, etc. Internet service is a good example of a very feature competitive and focused business. You can still set yourself apart by illustrating some of the benefits of their service.

If you have a great record of up-time, tell your potential customer about it and that they don't have to worry about losing sales when their sites are down as frequently as with other service- providers. In this example, the feature is the up-time, but the benefit is not losing sales and that helps your potential customers visualize why they might use your service. Someone may think up-time is just a number Internet service provides throw out there, but when they think, "Oh yeah, if it's not up,

I'm going to lose a sale," that's when it reaches your target market.

That's the kind of thing you want to talk to them about.

As another example, if you respond to support tickets or calls within an hour, you can say so. You can write about how you are the "stress-free Internet service provider that ensures your business can run as it should be 24-7". Again, the feature is having the response within an hour, but the benefit is less stress and again not missing out on important business time.

Exercise: Take that list of features you just created in the previous example and then list a benefit for each feature. This list will not only help you understand your product's benefit, but once you've done this exercise, you will have a large portion of the copy for your product done.

You can put that information in bullet point format onto your web page or brochure. And speaking of "bullets"…

Bullets

Bullets are one of the greatest things you'll come to love about copywriting. They are relatively easy to write and they can also sell your product exceptionally well.

The following are examples of bullet points:

What exactly a transcriptionist does and why her services are in such demand.

Perks of having your own transcriptionist business: Learn about the low start-up costs, how to set your own hours and work with the flexibility this business provides.

Bullets can be about the benefits of your products or the feature and often will include both just like I showed you in the previous two exercises.

Bullet points are an easy way to deliver a lot of information about your product, efficiently and effectively to your prospect. If you formatted all this information into paragraph format, they might not read it as readily.

Bullet points can also "tease" your readers into having more interest for your product. This is particularly effective when you're selling an informational product, course or book. A good bullet point teases about what's included and gets them excited to buy, but doesn't give away the actual information you're selling. You don't want to give your product away for free, of course!

For example (This is a purely fictional, of course!):
Bad bullet point:

Passionately kiss your husband each morning and he's sure to stay faithful.

Good bullet point:

Do this one thing each morning and your husband's eyes will never stray to another woman.

The first bullet point gives away what's in your information product. The other one tells the BENEFIT of what's included (the faithful husband), but doesn't tell you how to do it.

Headlines:

Your headline belongs at the top of your sales letter, web page, ad or any copy you are creating. Capitalize all the words in your headline and make it nice and big and bold to ensure it gets attention.

All good copy has an attention-getting headline. People are busy and you only have a limited amount of time to grab their attention. They won't read the small print on your page if you don't get their attention. A clear, benefit-oriented headline can help you do this.

A headline that simply says "We Sell X Widgets" doesn't say enough to get a reader to keep reading. Many people probably sell X Widgets. Why should they learn more about yours?

If you are having trouble figuring out headlines to use, here are a few headline starters. These are very common ones that are proven to work and you can try them out for your copy or do something completely different. These are just a way to start getting your mind going:

"Who Else Wants to   "

This is an easy way to start; relate to your audience.

An example: "Who Else Wants to Save Up to 50% on Their Phone Bill? Try Our Rates Calculator to Find the Best Deals on Long Distance. "

"How Made me and It Can Help You Too"

An example: "How X-Brand Weight-Loss Shake Made Me Lose 37 Pounds in 7 Weeks"

"Are You ?"

An example: "Are You Tired of Unsightly Bags under Your Eyes? Apply Just a Dab of X Cream Once a Day for 6 Days and Watch the Puffiness Disappear. "

"The Secrets to "

Everybody loves secrets…tell them about yours.

An example: "The Secrets to Rekindling the Romance with Your Husband"

"Give Me   and I'll   "

An example: "Give me 15 Days and I'll turn Your Ever-Reluctant Child into an Avid Reader".

Tell them what they have to put in to it and what benefit they will get out of it.

More Tips for Creating Great Headlines: Another great way to find good headlines is simply looking at websites, brochures and other sales copy and see what grabs your attention. You can use some of those ideas in your own headlines.

Be Specific: In one of the headlines, we talked about losing 37 pounds in 7 weeks. The headline mentioned a certain product; the subject lost a certain amount of weight in a certain amount of time. Being specific is very important in headlines and copy, in general, because that's what really grabs attention.

Being vague and saying things like "reduce eye puffiness" may grab some attention but telling them how easy it is; "a dab of cream once a day for 6 days"… that's something people will say hey, I could do that. When you don't give them that extra information right away; they may not keep reading.

Exercise: Visit a few websites or read ads in a newspaper or magazine. See what grabs your attention. Can you incorporate those ideas into your headline?

Subheadlines:

Sub-headlines are additional headlines in your sales copy. Usually, subheadlines won't be as big as other headlines in your copy, but they'll be bold each word will be capitalized to get attention.

Subheadlines help break up your copy to make it easier to read. It also helps get the attention of people who are skimming, rather than reading your sales copy. Use sub- headlines to draw attention to important sections of your copy every couple of paragraphs. Be specific in your sub-headlines and use benefits too.

Example: If you have written promotional copy for your free weekly email newsletter, you'll want subheadlines to draw in the eyes to important parts of the copy.

When you are about to include some bullet points about what's included in your newsletter, you might have a subheadline that reads:

Here's What's Included in Your Free Subscription to XXXXX

Then, just before you introduce your subscription form, you can have a subheadline that says:

Claim Your Free Subscription by Completing the Simple Form Below

Those are simply examples and copy that is more than a couple of paragraphs can be broken up in that manner.

Exercise: If you have some longer copy written (or if you're about to write some) go back and see where you can insert subheadlines. Visually, you'll see how it draws your eyes in, will help skimmers find the information they are looking for and how it makes instructions clearer for your readers.

Testimonials

A testimonial is positive feedback from someone who has used your products. Testimonials can be one of your most powerful online marketing tools. When someone is looking to buy a product, she often seeks the opinion of someone else who has used the product, right? If you have testimonials from your previous customers presented in your marketing materials or website copy, you already have a head start on making the sale.

Warning: You need to make sure your testimonials are meaningful. Look at these testimonials and decide if they are believable or would make you interested in a product:

"I love it." - Jan

"This is the best ever."

"This is going to be a great product." - Jim Bob, Florida

As you can probably see, the above testimonials are quite meaningless and probably won't add much to your marketing message. Here are some problems:

It's nice that Jan loves the product, but we don't know why. Nor do we really know who she is or if she's a real person.

The second also doesn't explain why it's the best and we don't know who made these comments.

The last example at least has a full name "Jim Bob" and we know he's from Florida, but it looks like he hasn't even tried the product. He says it is "going to be a great product". Just asking someone to comment on what your product might be like isn't an effective use of a testimonial.

A testimonial should include concrete and believable detail:

Testimonials should include information about how your customer used the product and the specific results she achieved.

Testimonials should also provide as much information about the testimonial provider as possible. Consumers are a skeptical bunch and if you don't convince them "Jan" or "Jim Bob" are real, they might not believe your testimonials. Where possible, include:

Full names (first and last)

Location (city and state/province)

Photos - Before and after photos, if applicable, can be very effective

Other proof of results – For example, if your product helped a child's grade improve in school. You can show photos or scanned images of reports showing the improvement.

If you think your customers won't offer this information, you won't know until you ask. You might also give them a little gift in return for their details and feedback. It can be a coupon, sample pack or anything you'd like. Just be careful in wording your gift offer. Asking someone for positive feedback in return for a gift can be seen as a bribe and would likely be illegal. Gifts should be offered in return for any type of feedback – positive or negative.

The important thing is to get as much credible information as you can for your testimonials. 10 mediocre testimonials are not nearly as effective as 3 great ones. So, if fewer people say yes to offering their personal information, that's just fine.

Exercise: Set up a questionnaire for your customers and offer them a gift of a valuable coupon or sample in return for any feedback they provide. Even if you receive some negative feedback, this is your opportunity to view it as constructive criticism and see how you can improve your business.

How long have you been using our product?

How has XXXX improved since starting to use the product (X being the main benefit of your product)?

How do you use the product (ex. at work, to relieve pain, etc)?

How much time do you invest in using the product on a weekly basis?

What is the most helpful/useful part of the product?

What would you say to someone who is interested in buying the product?

What other information would you like to share with us?

A questionnaire is often more effective than simply asking for feedback. If people are happy with the product, they will say so, but don't often provide the meaningful detail you need for an effective testimonial.

If you receive positive feedback that is particularly useful as a testimonial, contact the person who gave it to you and ask if you can publish:

Their full name

Picture

City and State/Province

Any proof they have

Don't be shy in asking. You may have to explain the purpose of all the information. Tell them how proud you are of their success and you really want to showcase them a real-live success story.

Call-to-action:

Your call-to-action is what you ask you reader to do once they read your promotional copy. It can be something as simple as calling you for more information, signing up for your mailing list or buying your product. If you don't tell people what to do, they are less likely to do it. Even if your copy implies they should buy your product, if you don't ask for the sale, you won't make it as often.

Every piece of sales copy should have a call-to-action whether it's a page on your website, your business card or other piece of copywriting.

Examples: Here are some examples of a call-to-action:

Click a link to place an order

Call a 1-800 number to place an order

Call a number to hear a recorded message

Fill in a form to enter a sweepstakes

Enter a name and email address to subscribe

Make sure your call-to-action is written in enticing way. Make it sound easy; give them a sense of entitlement like:

"Click here to claim your instant access to XXXX"

In the above example you are giving them owner ship by saying, "claim your instant access". Claim gives them the feeling they already own it, but they just need to claim it. The word "your" has also been added to make them feel like they own it. "Instant access" makes it sound easy.

Here's another example:

"Simply enter your first name, email address and click 'Subscribe Me' and we'll send your first XXX tip immediately."

The above example give them the clear steps they need to make it happen and shows how easy it is and how quickly they'll get what they are looking for.

Exercise: Take a look at every page of promotional material you've written. Ensure it has a call-to-action. If it doesn't, fix it. If you are just getting started with your business, be sure to remember it as you design each business card, each and every page on your website, etc.

Offer

An offer is simply what you are selling/giving to your readers.

Example: You are selling a customized embroidered baby blanket. If your customer pays you $35, they will get a 3' x 3' blanket in the color of their choice, design of their choice and embroidered message up to 25 letters. Additional designs have an extra charge.

Another example: An offer doesn't have to involve the exchange of money. In return for a first name and email address, you might give out a subscription to free weekly email tips on growing and caring for a garden.

Your offer is related to your call-to-action, but they're not exactly the same thing. Your offer is what you will give in return for money or whatever you're asking for. The call-to-action is the specific instruction you give for your potential customer to accept your offer.

Exercise: Take some time to write out all the details of your own offer. Get specific like I mentioned in the examples above.

That's it for the terminology portion of this guide. Before you start making offers and giving a call-to-action, you need to understand a few more things first...

Tips for Writing Great Copy

Now that you have an understanding of some of the important terminology involved in copywriting and how you can make the most of those elements, here are some more tips to help you craft great copy.

Speak to Your Audience

Since the sales copy you write is to promote your own products, it's easy to make the mistake of talking about yourself in your copy too much. The problem is, your potential customer doesn't really care about you. They care about themselves, they want solutions to their problems and they want to know what you can do for them. You need to focus on your customer first.

A lot of sales copy is too focused on the business who is doing the selling: "We sell this…"

"We're great at this…"

"We believe in customer satisfaction…"

It's simple enough to change wording around to focus more on "you" and how you can help your potential customer. Turn it around and write things like this instead:

"Are you looking for…" "If you need reliable…"
"Your satisfaction is guaranteed…"

Exercise: Go through your copy and change many of the "we's" to "yous" and rewrite your copy based on the change in focus. When you're done, you'll see how much more of a connection you can make with your reader. In most cases you'll be saying essentially the same thing (ex. Saying, "We believe in customer satisfaction" is pretty much the same as, "Your satisfaction is guaranteed"), but the focus is on your potential customer.

Avoid Excessive Adjectives

Can you see what's wrong with the following copywriting example?

"The biggest and best e-book that will make you the happiest person on your block."

Here's the problem: Outside of the fact that it' pretty over-the-top with its claims, that sentence above is pretty meaningless. Nobody really cares if an ebook is the biggest and this sentence really doesn't say anything about why it's the best. Also, the word happiest is kind of meaningless. We all want to be happy, but if we are unhappy right now we have specific problems we need to have solved. Telling someone they're going to be happy doesn't answer much for them. They want to know HOW you're going to make them happy and how you'll make their specific problems go away.

The real problem with the sentence above is that it's filled with adjectives that don't give specifics. Adjectives describe nouns and they don't provide readers with good information. Make sure you answer these questions in your copy:

How are you the best

What makes you great

How do you care for your customer

That's what people want to know. If you use too many adjectives, it ends up sounding like too much hype and the meaningfulness is lost.

That doesn't mean you can't use adjectives in your copy. Of course, you're still going to use them, but your copy should be able to stand on it's own without all the extra words.

Exercise: If you want to see if your copy can stand up on its own, pick a couple paragraphs from your website or your entire page and remove all the adjectives. Does it still sound compelling? Is it selling your product?

If not, it's probably time to start working on being specific and we'll talk about that next.

Be Specific

I talked about this briefly when we wrote about headlines. Let's get into this more and really understand how being specific can help you sell more of your product.

Instead of saying you ARE the best, say WHY you are the best. Instead of saying you're fast; explain how fast and in what specific ways. Let's say, if you are a printing service and you provide fast printing, tell them on average how much time you need to finish a project. If you aren't willing to say how quickly you can complete a project, then you're probably not that quick and shouldn't be using that angle.

When we're talking about copy, we're giving people as much detailed information as possible so people can make an informed decision about a product, newsletter, or whatever our call to action is.

Have you ever been to a website and thought about buying a product, but you weren't 100% sure it had the features/benefits you needed? It happens all the time. A lot of product-sellers think they can slap up a picture and add a few words and watch the sales roll in.

Unfortunately, it doesn't work that way.

You simply can't give too much information about your product. Yes, you can be too wordy and put your reader to sleep, but if you're giving people information that they need to make a buying decision, there is no such thing as too much information. You want them to have all their questions answered and get them to buy.

Another good way to be specific is to quantify things. If you have an ebook, that has 37 ways to reduce your cholesterol, tell them there are 37 ways. Don't say there are "plenty of ways" or "this ebook is packed with ideas to help you lower your cholesterol". A specific number like 37 as opposed to a round number like 30 also tends to generate a better response. It's not completely clear why this occurs, but it's likely because round numbers might seem made up or estimated, but when you say 37 it puts a specific picture in their mind.

Exercise: Look at things you've written for your business. Where can you be more specific? What can you quantify?

Don't Worry So Much about Grammar

As you continue with your business, there will be people that tell you that proper grammar is very important to maintain a professional image. Some of your websites visitors may even take the time to email and tell you about the spelling and grammar mistakes that completely outraged them. Don't let this worry you too much. Correct the spelling and if the grammar is outrageous, fix it – but keep reading to find out why grammar isn't as important as it's cracked up to be.

The most important thing about your sales copy or articles is to sound natural and to relate to your target audience appropriately. Write the way you speak.

Naturally, if your audience is PHD students studying literature, then you might have to have a more formal tone and pay more attention to more grammar rules. If you're audience is race- car enthusiasts or those interested in fashion trends, you might be more relaxed in your writing and speak more casually.

Most markets are going to be more casual, so you want to create a friendly and real image with your copy. It's okay to start sometimes sentences with "and" and "but" now and then because it's how we speak and when you write how you speak, it's how you relate to your audience. It's ok to end a sentence with a preposition because, again, that's how we speak.

Exercise: Look at your copy and see how formal or informal you are. Can you see how you could make it sound more friendly, appealing and create a connection with your reader? If you're too formal, you might just lose your audience all together. You don't want to sound uneducated but you want to be natural. Most of your grammar is going to be correct, but there are some rules you don't necessarily have to worry about for the sake of readability.

Final Note: If you're going to have someone proofread your copy, whether it's a friend, virtual assistant or professional proofreader, make sure they understand what you are looking for; that your spelling is correct, the language flows well and the copy sounds intelligent but friendly.

Keep it Simple

Write in short sentences to make things easy to read. Break up long paragraphs to ease eye- strain. Again, it's okay to break grammar rules – especially with paragraph formatting because reading long paragraphs can be fatiguing. This is particularly true online and where people are reading on a screen. Don't tire your potential customer out before they read about your product.

You can also bullet points, as we mentioned earlier, and these may include incomplete sentences. Luckily that is actually acceptable in grammar rules! The key is to make it easy to read.

Don't use complicated language and make the level appropriate for your target audience. The average reading level of the general public is quite low. If you feel a more advanced word is more appropriate always define the word, in case your readers don't know what it means.

Keep Layouts Simple

It's easy to get excited about your product and when crafting your website design, it can be tempting to include so many things. Add photos to accentuate the copy, but don't allow them to take over. Pictures are important in creating visuals, but it's your words that will make your copy sell.

On the Internet, keeping it simple is especially important. Web surfers only give you a few seconds before they decide to click away and never to come back to your website again. If you don't grab attention or you confuse them with a busy website, they are more likely to make that decision to leave.

Here are some important tips for your website layouts:

Keep your website navigation to a minimum. Create sub-categories to your website sections if necessary to minimize menu distractions.

If you're selling your own product on a particular page, it's usually best to remove all banners or graphics going to outside pages.

Keep your page header or logo simple and small. Don't let it take over the whole "above-the-fold" space on your website. "Above-the-fold" simply means the space on your web page a visitor can see without scrolling down with her mouse.

A logo or page header can help with branding and can convey a more professional image, but it doesn't have to be huge to do that. Most of the above- the-fold space should be reserved for selling your product.

Exercise: Review your web pages and promotional copy and try to view it from the eyes of someone who is unfamiliar with you, your company or your product. Are you immediately able to receive the intended marketing message or are their other distractions on the page? Try to clean things up and then ask others for honest feedback.

Note about Sales Letters: If you've been online any amount of time, you've probably seen web pages called "sales letters". They're the long scrolling pages with a headline, information about the product and a call-to-action.

The types of pages are very effective when selling one product at a time. The reasons they are effective are because:

They have no distractions. There's no navigation (except maybe on the bottom), flashing banners or anything to keep attention away from the product.

Everything is in one place. The reader doesn't have to click around, trying to find the information they need.

It includes everything your visitor needs to know to make a decision about buying your product.

Note about Opt-In Pages: In addition to sales letters selling individual products, you've probably come across what's called an "Opt-In Page". It is similar to a sales letter in that there are no distractions and navigation, but the purpose of this page is to get them sign up for a mailing list or opt-in for more information on a product, etc.

These are highly effective in building your mailing list and can have extremely high conversion rates. They're perfect for promoting on your business card, in a forum or email signature or anywhere you want to draw people in with your free information to sell to them later.

Again, if you chose the full version of this course and software, you have access to my Opt- In Page Builder software. The software and guide that is in your download area will give you more information on when to use these types of pages and how to make the most of them.

Be Succinct & Edit

Earlier, we told you how important it is to provide as much information about your product, so that your customer can make an informed buying decision. We still stand by that, but we want you to also be as succinct (using only as many words as necessary) in your copy as possible.

There's a difference between summarizing your offer and just repeating yourself over and over again. Although it's true that detail is what really sells your product, you want to make sure your copy is succinct and receives proper editing attention.

Exercise: Go through your copy and make sure that you're not being repetitive or adding extra information your potential customer doesn't need. If you start out with really long copy, go over it over and over again, until you've fine-tuned it into a well-oiled selling machine. It's not the length that can be a problem, but the message you are sending with your copy.

Sense of Urgency – Get Them to Buy Now

Even though people may be excited about your product after reading about it, they may just decide they'll buy later. Problem is, most times when they decide to buy later; they never get around to it. They'll lose your brochure, throw out the newspaper with your ad or forget where your website is.

To prevent this, you need to create a sense of urgency. In other words, make them feel like they need to buy now. Here are some ways you can make them feel like buying now:

Offer a time-limited discount

Limit the distribution of your product

Offer them extra bonuses or goodies with your product, but only for a limited time.

Show them how serious there particular problem is and why they should find a solution now

Whatever you can do to make them purchase now, the more likely you'll make the sale.

Exercise: Go through your promotional material and make sure you've added a sense of urgency to everything. Whether it's to encourage them to find a solution to their problem now or to offer a time-limited discount, you can always add a little sense of urgency.

Close the Deal – Call-to-Action

Never forget to ask for the sale. Or if you want people to call you for more information, fill out of a form or sign up for a mailing list, tell them exactly what you want to do. We defined the call-to-action in the previous section, but it's definitely worth mentioning again.

Your call-to-action can include:

A summary of your offer.

Your price and why the price provides good value.

Specific instruction on how to complete the call to action.

In the previous 2 chapters, I've provided you with the foundations of what it takes to write effective sales copy. If you already have an established business, you have plenty of opportunities to go back and improve your sales messages. If you are just getting started, you are already ahead of much of your competition. Most website owners don't really understand copywriting and rely on more person-to-person selling and follow-up. With the skills you're learning now, you'll have your website doing most of the selling for you.

Putting it All Together

Copywriting helps you clinch a sale when you're not there to do it. When people visit your website, you aren't there to personally greet them. When someone looks at your business card a few weeks after they meet you, how will they remember you?

Use the copywriting basics to guide you in crafting all your marketing messages. The words on your page, on your business card or in your advertising copy say a lot about you and your business. Make sure you're sending the right message.

If you haven't already, go through all the exercises in this guide and see the differences they can make in your business. Knowledge is power, but without action...it's almost useless.

Printed by Libri Plureos GmbH in Hamburg,
Germany